Sappho and Phaon

Mary Robinson

DODO
PRESS

SAPPHO AND PHAON
IN A
SERIES
OF
Legitimate Sonnets,
WITH
THOUGHTS ON POETICAL SUBJECTS,
AND
ANECDOTES
OF THE
GRECIAN POETESS.

BY
MARY ROBINSON,
Author of Poems, &c. &c. &c. &c.

1796.

PREFACE

IT must strike every admirer of poetical compositions, that the modern sonnet, concluding with two lines, winding up the sentiment of the whole, confines the poet's fancy, and frequently occasions an abrupt termination of a beautiful and interesting picture; and that the ancient, or what is generally denominated, the LEGITIMATE SONNET, may be carried on in a series of sketches, composing, in parts, one historical or imaginary subject, and forming in the whole a complete and connected story.

With this idea, I have ventured to compose the following collection; not presuming to offer them as imitations of PETRARCH, but as specimens of that species of sonnet writing, so seldom attempted in the English language; though adopted by that sublime Bard, whose Muse produced the grand epic of Paradise Lost, and the humbler effusion, which I produce as an example of the measure to which I allude, and which is termed by the most classical writers, the legitimate sonnet.

O Nightingale, that on yon bloomy spray
Warblest at eve, when all the woods are still,
Thou with fresh hope the lover's heart dost fill,
While the jolly hours lead on propitious May.
Thy liquid notes that close the eye of day
First heard before the shallow cuccoo's bill,
Portend succes in love; O if Jove's will
Have link'd that amorous power to thy soft lay,
Now timely sing, ere the rude bird of hate

Foretel my hopeless doom in some grove nigh,
As thou from year to year hast sung too late
For my relief, yet hadst no reason why:
Whether the Muse, or Love call thee his mate,
Both them I serve, and of their train am I.

To enumerate the variety of authors who have written sonnets of all descriptions, would be endless; indeed few of them deserve notice: and where, among the heterogeneous mass of insipid and laboured efforts, sometimes a bright gem sheds lustre on the page of poesy, it scarcely excites attention, owing to the disrepute in which sonnets are fallen. So little is rule attended to by many, who profess the art of poetry, that I have seen a composition of more than thirty lines, ushered into the world under the name of Sonnet, and that, from the pen of a writer, whose classical taste ought to have avoided such a misnomer.

Doctor Johnson describes a Sonnet, as "a short poem, consisting of fourteen lines, of which the rhymes are adjusted by a particular rule." He further adds, "It has not been used by any man of eminence since MILTON." Sensible of the extreme difficulty I shall have to encounter, in offering to the world a little wreath, gathered in that path, which, even the best poets have thought it dangerous to tread; and knowing that the English language is, of all others, the least congenial to such an undertaking, (for, I believe, that the construction of this kind of sonnet was originally in the Italian, where the vowels are used almost every other letter,) I only point out the track where more able pens may follow with success; and where the most classical beauties may be adopted, and drawn forth with peculiar advantage.

Sophisticated sonnets are so common, for every rhapsody of rhyme, from six lines to sixty comes under that denomination, that the eye frequently turns from this species of poem with disgust. Every school-boy, every romantic scribbler, thinks a sonnet a task of little difficulty. From this ignorance in some, and vanity in others, we see the monthly and diurnal publications abounding with ballads, odes, elegies, epitaphs, and allegories, the non-descript ephemera from the heated brains of self-important poetasters, all ushered into notice under the appellation of SONNET!

I confess myself such an enthusiastic votary of the Muse, that any innovation which seems to threaten even the least of her established rights, makes me tremble, lest that chaos of dissipated pursuits which has too long been growing like an overwhelming shadow, and menacing the lustre of intellectual light, should, aided by the idleness of some, and the profligacy of others, at last obscure the finer mental powers, and reduce the dignity of talents to the lowest degradation.

As poetry has the power to raise, so has it also the magic to refine. The ancients considered the art of such importance, that before they led forth their heroes to the most glorious enterprizes, they animated them by the recital of grand and harmonious compositions. The wisest scrupled not to reverence the invocations of minds, graced with the charm of numbers: so mystically fraught are powers said to be, which look beyond the surface of events, that an admired and classical writer, describing the inspirations of the MUSE, thus expresses his opinion:

> So when remote futurity is brought
> Before the keen inquiry of her thought,
> A terrible sagacity informs
> The Poet's heart, he looks to distant storms,
> He hears the thunder ere the tempest low'rs,
> And, arm'd with strength surpassing human pow'rs,
> Seizes events as yet unknown to man,
> And darts his soul into the dawning plan.
> Hence in a Roman mouth the graceful name
> Of Prophet and of Poet was the same,
> Hence British poets too the priesthood shar'd,
> And ev'ry hallow'd druid—was a bard."

That poetry ought to be cherished as a national ornament, cannot be more strongly exemplified than in the simple fact, that, in those centuries when the poets' laurels have been most generously fostered in Britain, the minds and manners of the natives have been most polished and enlightened. Even the language of a country refines into purity by the elegance of numbers: the strains of WALLER have done more to effect that, then all the labours of monkish pedantry, since the days of druidical mystery and superstition.

Though different minds are variously affected by the infinite diversity of harmonious effusions, there are, I believe, very few that are wholly insensible to the powers of poetic compositions. Cold must that bosom be, which can resist the magical versification of Eloisa to Abelard; and torpid to all the more exalted sensations of the soul is that being, whose ear is not delighted by the grand and sublime effusions of the divine Milton! The romantic chivalry of Spencer vivifies the imagination; while the plaintive sweetness of Collins soothes and penetrates the heart. How much would Britain have been defecit in a comparison with other countries on the scale of intellectual grace, had these poets never existed! yet it is a melancholy truth, that here, where the attributes of genius have been diffused by the liberal hand of nature, almost to prodigality, there has not been, during a long series of years, the smallest mark of public distinction bestowed on literary talents. Many individuals, whose works are held in the highest estimation, now that their ashes sleep in the sepulchre, were, when living, suffered to languish, and even to perish, in obscure poverty: as if it were the peculiar fate of genius, to be neglected while existing, and only honoured when the consciousness of inspiration is vanished for ever.

The ingenious mechanic has the gratification of seeing his labours patronized, and is rewarded for his invention while he has the powers of enjoying its produce. But the Poet's life is one perpetual scene of warfare: he is assailed by envy, stung by malice, and wounded by the fastidious comments of concealed assassins. The more eminently beautiful his compositions are, the larger is the phalanx he has to encounter; for the enemies of genius are multitudinous.

It is the interest of the ignorant and powerful, to suppress the effusions of enlightened minds: when only monks could write, and nobles read, authority rose triumphant over fright; and the slave, spell-bound in ignorance, hugged his fetters without repining. It was then that the best powers of reason lay buried like the gem in the dark mine; by a slow and tedious progress they have been drawn forth, and must, ere long, diffuse an universal lustre: for that era is rapidly advancing, when talents will tower like an unperishable column, while the globe will be strewed with the wrecks of superstition.

As it was the opinion of the ancients, that poets possessed the powers of prophecy, the name was consequently held in the most unbounded veneration. In less remote periods the bard has been publicly distinguished; princes and priests have bowed before the majesty of genius: Petrarch was crowned with laurels, the noblest diadem, in the Capitol of Rome: his admirers were liberal, his contemporaries were just; and his name will stand upon record, with the united and honourable testimony of his own talents, and the generosity of his country.

It is at once a melancholy truth, and a national disgrace, that this Island, so profusely favored bynature, should be marked, of all enlightened countries, as the most neglectful of literary merit! and I will venture to believe, that there are both POETS and PHILOSOPHERS, now living in Britain, who, had they been born in any other clime, would have been honoured with the proudest distinctions, and immortalized to the latest posterity.

I cannot conclude these opinions without paying tribute to the talents of my illustrious country-women; who, unpatronized by the courts, and unprotected by the powerful, persevere in the paths of literature, and ennoble themselves by the unperishable lustre of MENTAL PRE-EMINENCE!

TO THE READER.

The story of the *LESBIAN MUSE,* though not new to the classical reader, presented to my imagination such a lively example of the human mind, enlightened by the most exquisite talents, yet yielding to the destructive controul of ungovernable passions, that I felt an irresistible impulse to attempt the delineation of their progress; mingling with the glowing picture of her soul, such moral reflections, as may serve to exite that pity, which, while it proves the susceptibility of the heart, arms it against the danger of indulging too luxuriant fancy.

The unfortunate lovers, Heloise and Abelard; and, the supposed platonic, Petrarch and Laura, have found panegyrists in many distinguished authors. *OVID* and *POPE* have celebrated the passion of Sappho for Phaon; but their portraits, however beautifully finished, are replete with shades, tending rather to depreciate than to adorn the Grecian Poetess.

I have endeavoured to collect, in the succeeding pages, the mostliberal accounts of that illustrious woman, whose fame has transmitted to us some fragments of her works, through many dark ages, and for the space of more than two thousand years. The merit of her compositions must have been indisputable, to have left all cotemporary female writers in obscurity; for it is known, that poetry was, at the period in which she lived, held in the most sacred veneration; and that those who were gifted with that divine inspiration, were ranked as the first class of human beings.

Among the many Grecian writers, Sappho was the unrivalled poetess of her time: the envy she excited, the public honours she received, and the fatal passion which terminated her existence, will, I trust, create that sympathy in the mind of the susceptible reader, which may render the following poetical trifles not wholly uninteresting.

MARY ROBINSON
St. James's Place,
1796.

ACCOUNT OF SAPPHO.

SAPPHO, whom the ancients distinguished by the title of the TENTH MUSE, was born at Mytilene in the island of Lesbos, six hundred years before the Christian era. As no particulars have been transmitted to posterity, respecting the origin of her family, it is most likely she derived by little consequence from birth of connection. At an early period of her life she was wedded to Cercolus, a native of the isle of Andros; he was possessed of considerable wealth, and though the Lesbian Muse is said to have been sparingly gifted with beauty, he became enamoured of her, more perhaps on account of mental, than personal charms. By this union she is said to have given birth to a daughter; but Cercolus leaving her, while young, in a state of widowhood, she never after could be prevailed on to marry.

The Fame which her genius spread even to the remotest parts of the earth, excited the envy of some writers who endeavoured to throw over her private character, a shade, which shrunk before the brilliancy of her poetical talents. Her soul was replete with harmony, that harmony which neither art nor study can acquire; she felt the intuitive superiority, and to the Muses she paid unbounded adoration.

The Mytilenians held her poetry in such high veneration, and were so sensible of the hour conferred on the country which gave her birth, that they coined money with the impression of her head; and at the time of her death, paid tribute to their memory, such as was offered to sovereigns only.

The story of Antiochus has been related as an unequivocal proof of Sappho's skill in discovering, and powers of describing the passions of the human mind. That prince is said to have entertained a fatal affection for his mother-in-law Stratonice; which, though he endeavoured to subdue it's influence, preyed upon his frame, and after many ineffectual struggles, at length reduced him to extreme danger. His physicians marked the symptoms attending his malady, and found them so exactly correspond with Sappho's delineation of the tender passion, that they did not hesitate to form a decisive opinion of the cause, which had produced so perilous an effect.

That Sappho was not insensible to the feelings she so well described , is evident in her writings but it was scarcely possible, that a mind so exquisitely tender, so sublimely gifted, should escape those fascinations which even apathy itself has been awakened to acknowledge.

The scarce specimens now extant, from the pen of the Grecian Muse, have by the most competent judges been esteemed as the standard for the pathetic, the glowing, and the amatory. The ode, which has been so highly estimated, is written in a measure distinguished by the title of the Sapphic. POPE made it his model in his juvenile production, beginning—

"Happy the man—whose wish and care"—

Addison was opinion, that the writings of Sappho were replete with such fascinating beauties, and adorned with such a vivid glow of sensibility, that, probably, had they been preserved entire, it would have been dangerous to have perused them. They possessed none of the artificial decorations of a feigned passion; they were the genuine effusions of a supremely enlightened soul, laboring to subdue a fatal enchantment; and vainly opposing the conscious pride of illustrious fame, against the warm susceptibility of a generous bosom.

Though few stanzas from the pen of the Lesbian poetess have darted through the shades of oblivion: yet, those that remain are so exquisitely touching and beautiful, that they prove beyond dispute the taste, feeling, and inspiration of the mind which produced them. In examining the curiosities of antiquity, we look to the perfections, and not the magnitude of those relics, which have been preserved amidst the wrecks of time: as the smallest gem that bears the fine touches of a master, surpasses the loftiest fabric reared by the labours of false taste, so the precious fragments of the immortal Sappho, will be admired, when the voluminous productions of inferior poets are mouldered into dust.

When it is considered, that the few specimens we have of the poems of the Grecian Muse, have passed through three and twenty centuries, and consequently through the hands of innumerable translators: and when it is known that Envy frequently delights in the base occupation of depreciating merit which it canot aspire to emulate; it may be conjectured, that some passages are erroneously given to posterity, either by ignorance or design. Sappho, whose fame beamed round her with the superior effulgence which her works had created, knew that she was writing for future ages; it is not therefore natural that she should produce any composition which might tend to tarnish her reputation, or lessen that celebrity which it was the labour of her life to consecrate. The delicacy of her sentiments cannot find a more eloquent advocate than in her own effusions; she is said to have commended in the most animated panegyric, the virtues of her brother Lanychus; and with the most pointed and severe censure, to have contemned the passion which her prother Charaxus entertained for the beautiful Rhodope. If her writings were, in some instances, too glowing for the fastidious refinement of modern times; let it be her excuse, and the honour of her country, that the liberal education of the Greeks was such, as inspired them with an unprejudiced enthusiasm for the works of genius: and that when they paid adoration to Sappho, they idolized the MUSE, and not the WOMAN.

I shall conclude this account with an extract from the works of the learned and enlightened Abbe' Barthelemi; at once the vindication and eulogy of the Grecian Poetess.

"Sappho undertook to inspire the Lesbian women with a taste for literature; many of them received instructions from her, and foreign women increased the number of her disciples. She loved them to excess, because it was impossible for her to love otherwise; and she expressed her tenderness in all the violence of passion: your surprize at this will cease, when you are acquainted with the extreme sensibility of the Greeks; and discover, that amongst them the most innocent connections often borrow the impassioned language of love.

"A certain facility of manners, she possessed; and the warmth of her expressions were but too well calculated to expose her to the hatred of some women of distinction, humbled by her superiority; and the jealousy of some of her disciples, who happened to be the objects of her preference. To this hatred she replied by truths and irony, which completely exasperated her enemies. She repaired to Sicily, where a statue was erected to her; it was sculptured by SILANION, one of the most celebrated staturists of his time. The sensibility of SAPPHO was extreme! she loved PHAON, who forsook her; after various efforts to bring him back, she took the leap of Leucata, and perished in the waves!

"Death has not obliterated the stain imprinted on her character; for ENVY, which fastens on ILLUSTRIOUS NAMES, does not expire; but bequeaths her aspersions to that calumny which NEVER DIES.

"Several Grecian women have cultivated POETRY, with success, but none have hitherto attained to the excellence of SAPPHO. And among other poets, there are few, indeed, who have surpassed her."

THE *SUBJECT* OF EACH SONNET.

~~~~~~
~~~~~~

"FLENDUS AMOR MEUS EST; ELEGEIA FLEBILE CARMEN;
NON FACIT AD LACRYMAS BARBITOS ULLA MEAS."
Ovid.

"Love taught my tears in sadder notes to flow,
And tun'd my heart to elegies of woe."
Pope.

SONNET INTRODUCTORY

~~~~~~~~~~~~~~~~

FAVOUR'D by Heav'n are those, ordain'd to taste
The bliss supreme that kindles fancy's fire;
Whose magic fingers sweep the muses' lyre,
In varying cadence, eloquently chaste!
Well may the mind, with tuneful numbers grac'd,
To Fame's immortal attributes aspire,
Above the treach'rous spells of low desire,
That wound the sense, by vulgar joys debas'd.
For thou, blest POESY! with godlike pow'rs
To calm the miseries of man wert giv'n;
When passion rends, and hopeless love devours,
By mem'ry goaded, and by frenzy driv'n,
'Tis thine to guide him 'midst Elysian bow'rs,
And shew his fainting soul,—a glimpse of Heav'n.

SONNET II.

~~~~~~~~~~~~~~~~

HIGH on a rock, coaeval with the skies,
A Temple stands, rear'd by immortal pow'rs
To Chastity divine! ambrosial flow'rs
Twining round icicles, in columns rise,
Mingling with pendent gems of orient dyes!
Piercing the air, a golden crescent tow'rs,
Veil'd by transparent clouds; while smiling hours
Shake from their varying wings—celestial joys!
The steps of spotless marble, scatter'd o'er
With deathless roses arm'd with many a thorn,
Lead to the altar. On the frozen floor,
Studded with tear-drops petrified by scorn,
Pale vestals kneel the Goddess to adore,
While Love, his arrows broke, retires forlorn.

SONNET III.

~~~~~~~~~~~~~~~~

TURN to yon vale beneath, whose tangled shade
Excludes the blazing torch of noon-day light,
Where sportive Fawns, and dimpled Loves invite,
The bow'r of Pleasure opens to the glade:
Lull'd by soft flutes, on leaves of violets laid,
There witching beauty greets the ravish'd sight,
More gentle than the arbitress of night
In all her silv'ry panoply array'd!
The birds breathe bliss! light zephyrs kiss the ground,
Stealing the hyacinth's divine perfume;
While from the pellucid fountains glitt'ring round,
Small tinkling rills bid rival flow'rets bloom!
HERE, laughing Cupids bathe the bosom's wound;
THERE, tyrant passion finds a glorious tomb!

SONNET IV

~~~~~~~~~~~~~~~~

WHY, when I gaze on Phaon's beauteous eyes,
Why does each thought in wild disorder stray?
Why does each fainting faculty decay,
And my chill'd breast in throbbing tumults rise?
Mute, on the ground my Lyre neglected lies,
The Muse forgot, and lost the melting lay;
My down-cast looks, my faultering lips betray,
That stung by hopeless passion,—Sappho dies!
Now, on a bank of Cypress let me rest;
Come, tuneful maids, ye pupils of my care,
Come, with your dulcet numbers soothe my breast;
And, as the soft vibrations float on air,
Let pity waft my spirit to the blest,
To mock the barb'rous triumphs of despair!

SONNET V.

~~~~~~~~~~~~~~

O! How can LOVE exulting Reason queil!
How fades each nobler passion from his gaze!
E'en Fame, that cherishes the Poet's lays,
That fame, ill-fated Sappho lov'd so well.
Lost is the wretch, who in his fatal spell
Wastes the short Summer of delicious days,
And from the tranquil path of wisdom strays,
In passion's thorny wild, forlorn to dwell.
O ye! who in that sacred Temple smile
Where holy Innocence resides enshrin'd;
Who fear not sorrow, and who know not guile,
Each thought compos'd, and ev'ry wish resign'd;
Tempt not the path where pleasure's flow'ry wile
In sweet, but pois'nous fetters, holds the mind.

SONNET VI.

~~~~~~~~~~~~~~~~

IS it to love, to fix the tender gaze,
To hide the timid blush, and steal away;
To shun the busy world, and waste the day
In some rude mountain's solitary maze?
Is it to chant *one* name in ceaseless lays,
To hear no words that other tongues can say,
To watch the pale moon's melancholy ray,
To chide in fondness, and in folly praise?
Is it to pour th' involuntary sigh,
To dream of bliss, and wake new pangs to prove;
To talk, in fancy, with the speaking eye,
Then start with jealousy, and wildly rove;
Is it to loathe the light, and wish to die?
For these I feel,—and feel that they are Love.

SONNET VII.

~~~~~~~~~~~~~~~~~

COME, Reason, come! each nerve rebellious bind,
Lull the fierce tempest of my fev'rish soul;
Come, with the magic of thy meek controul,
And check the wayward wand'rings of my mind:
Estrang'd from thee, no solace can I find,
O'er my rapt brain, where pensive visions stole,
Now passion reigns and stormy tumults roll—
So the smooth Sea obeys the furious wind!
In vain Philosophy unfolds his store,
O'erwhelm'd is ev'ry source of pure delight;
Dim is the golden page of wisdom's lore;
All nature fades before my sick'ning sight:
For what bright scene can fancy's eye explore,
'Midst dreary labyrinths of mental night?

SONNET VIII.

~~~~~~~~~~~~~~~~~

WHY, through each aching vein, with lazy pace
Thus steals the languid fountain of my heart,
While, from its source, each wild convulsive start
Tears the scorch'd roses from my burning face?
In vain, O Lesbian Vales! your charms I trace;
Vain is the poet's theme, the sculptor's art;
No more the Lyre its magic can impart,
Though wak'd to sound, with more than mortal grace!
Go, tuneful maids, go bid my Phaon prove
That passion mocks the empty boast of fame;
Tell him no joys are sweet, but joys of love,
Melting the soul, and thrilling all the frame!
Oh! may th'ecstatic thought in bosom move,
And sighs of rapture, fan the blush of shame!

SONNET IX.

~~~~~~~~~~~~~~~~

YE, who in alleys green and leafy bow'rs,
Sport, the rude children of fantastic birth;
Where frolic nymphs, and shaggy tribes of mirth,
In clam'rous revels waste the midnight hours;
Who, link'd in flaunting bands of mountain flow'rs,
Weave your wild mazes o'er the dewy earth,
Ere the fierce Lord of Lustre rushes forth,
And o'er the world his beamy radiance pours!
Oft has your clanking cymbal's madd'ning strain,
Loud ringing through the torch-illumin'd grove,
Lur'd my lov'd Phaon from the youthful train,
Through rugged dells, o'er craggy rocks to rove;
Then how can she his vagrant heart detain,
Whose Lyre throbs only to the touch of Love!

SONNET X.

~~~~~~~~~~~~~~~~

DANG'ROUS to hear, is that melodious tongue,
And fatal to the sense those murd'rous eyes,
Where in a sapphire sheath, Love's arrow lies,
Himself conceal'd the crystal haunts among!
Oft o'er that form, enamour'd have I hung,
On that smooth cheek to mark the deep'ning dyes,
While from that lip the fragrant breath would rise,
That lip, like Cupid's bow with rubies strung!
Still let me gaze upon that polish'd brow,
O'er which the golden hair luxuriant plays;
So, on the modest lily's leaves of snow
The proud Sun revels in resplendent rays!
Warm as his beams this sensate heart shall glow,
Till life's last hour, with Phaon's self decays!

SONNET XI.

~~~~~~~~~~~~~~~~

O! Reason! vaunted Sovreign of the mind!
Thou pompous vision with a sounding name!
Can'st thou, the soul's rebellious passions tame!
Can'st thou in spells the vagrant fancy bind?
Ah, no! capricious as the wav'ring wind,
Are sighs of Love that dim thy boasted flame,
While Folly's torch consumes the wreath of fame,
And Pleasure's hands the sheaves of truth unbind.
Press'd by the storms of Fate, hope shrinks and dies;
Frenzy darts forth in mightiest ills array'd;
Around thy throne destructive tumults rise,
And hell-fraught jealousies, thy rights invade!
Then, what art thou? O! Idol of the wise!
A visionary theme!—a gorgeous shade!

SONNET XII.

~~~~~~~~~~~~~~~~

NOW, o'er the tessellated pavement strew
Fresh saffron, steep'd in essence of the rose,
While down yon agate column gently flows
A glitt'ring streamlet of ambrosial dew!
My Phaon smiles! the rich carnation's hue,
On his flush'd cheek in conscious lustre glows,
While o'er his breast enamour'd Venus throws
Her starry mantle of celestial blue!
Breathe soft, ye dulcet flutes, among the trees
Where clust'ring boughs with golden citron twine;
While slow vibrations, dying on the breeze,
Shall soothe his soul with harmony divine!
Then let my form his yielding fancy seize,
And all his fondest wishes, blend with mine.

SONNET XIII.

~~~~~~~~~~~~~~~~

BRING, bring to deck my brow, ye Sylvan girls,
A roseate wreath; nor for my waving hair
The costly band of studded gems prepare,
Of sparkling crysolite or orient pearls:
Love, o'er my head his canopy unfurls,
His purple pinions fan the whisp'ring air;
Mocking the golden sandal, rich and rare,
Beneath my feet the fragrant woodbine curls.
Bring the thin robe, to fold about my breast,
White as the downy swan; while round my waist
Let leaves of glossy myrtle bind the vest,
Not idly gay, but elegantly chaste!
Love scorns the nymph in wanton trappings drest;
And charms the most concealed, are doubly grac'd.

SONNET XIV.

~~~~~~~~~~~~~~~~

COME, soft Aeolian harp, while zephyr plays
Along the meek vibration of thy strings,
As twilight's hand her modest mantle brings,
Blending with sober grey, the western blaze!
O! prompt my Phaon's dreams with tend'rest lays,
Ere night o'er shade thee with its humid wings,
While the lorn Philomel his sorrow sings
In leafy cradle, red with parting rays!
Slow let thy dulcet tones on ether glide,
So steals the murmur of the am'rous dove;
The mazy legions swarm on ev'ry side,
To lulling sounds the sunny people move!
Let not the wise their little world deride,
The smallest sting can wound the breast of Love.

SONNET XV.

~~~~~~~~~~~~~~~

NOW, round my favor'd grot let roses rise,
To strew the bank where Phaon wakes from rest;
O! happy buds! to kiss his burning breast,
And die, beneath the lustre of his eyes!
Now, let the timbrels echo to the skies,
Now damsels sprinkel cassia on his vest,
With od'rous wreaths of constant myrtle drest,
And flow'rs, deep tinted with the rainbow's dyes!
From cups of porphyry let nectar flow,
Rich as the perfume of Phoenicia's vine!
Now let his dimpling cheek with rapture glow,
While round his heart love's mystic fetters twine;
And let the Grecian Lyre its aid bestow,
In songs of triumph, to proclaim him mine!

SONNET XVI.

~~~~~~~~~~~~~~~

DELUSIVE Hope! more transient than the ray
That leads pale twilight to her dusky bed,
O'er woodland glen, or breezy mountain's head,
Ling'ring to catch the parting sigh of day.
Hence with thy visionary charms, away!
Nor o'er my path the flow'rs of fancy spread;
Thy airy dreams on peaceful pillows shed,
And weave for thoughtless brows, a garland gay.
Farewell low vallies; dizzy cliffs, farewell!
Small vagrant rills that murmur as ye flow:
Dark bosom'd labyrinth and thorny dell;
The task be mine all pleasures to forego;
To hide, where meditation loves to dwell,
And feed my soul, with luxury of woe!

SONNET XVII.

~~~~~~~~~~~~~~~~

Love steals unheeded o'er the tranquil mind,
As Summer breezes fan the sleeping main,
Slow through each fibre creeps the subtle pain,
'Till closely round the yielding bosom twin'd.
Vain is the hope the magic to unbind,
The potent mischief riots in the brain,
Grasps ev'ry thought, and burns in ev'ry vein,
'Till in the heart the Tyrant lives enshrin'd.
Oh! Victor strong! bending the vanquish'd frame;
Sweet is the thraldom that thou bid'st us prove!
And sacred is the tear thy victims claim,
For blest are those whom sighs of sorrow move!
Then nymphs beware how ye profane my name,
Nor blame my weakness, till like me ye love!

SONNET XVIII.

~~~~~~~~~~~~~~~~

WHY art thou chang'd? O Phaon! tell me why?
Love flies reproach, when passion feels decay;
Or, I would paint the raptures of that day,
When, in sweet converse, mingling sigh with sigh,
I mark'd the graceful languor of thine eye
As on a shady bank entranc'd we lay:
O! Eyes! whose beamy radiance stole away
As stars fade trembling from the burning sky!
Why art thou chang'd? dear source of all my woes!
Though dark my bosom's tint, through ev'ry vein
A ruby tide of purest lustre flows,
Warm'd by thy love, or chill'd by thy disdain;
And yet no bliss this sensate Being knows;
Ah! why is rapture so allied to pain?

SONNET XIX.

~~~~~~~~~~~~~~~~

FAREWELL, ye coral caves, ye pearly sands,
Ye waving woods that crown yon lofty steep;
Farewell, ye Nereides of the glitt'ring deep,
Ye mountain tribes, ye fawns, ye sylvan bands:
On the bleak rock your frantic minstrel stands,
Each task forgot, save that, to sigh and weep;
In vain the strings her burning fingers sweep,
No more her touch, the Grecian Lyre commands!
In Circe's cave my faithless Phaon's laid,
Her daemons dress his brow with opiate flow'rs;
Or, loit'ring in the brown pomgranate shade,
Beguile with am'rous strains the fateful hours;
While Sappho's lips, to paly ashes fade,
And sorrow's cank'ring worm her heart devours!

SONNET XX.

~~~~~~~~~~~~~~~~

OH! I could toil for thee o'er burning plains;
Could smile at poverty's disastrous blow;
With thee, could wander 'midst a world of snow,
Where one long night o'er frozen Scythia reigns.
Sever'd from thee, my sick'ning soul disdains
The thrilling thought, the blissful dream to know,
And can'st thou give my days to endless woe,
Requiting sweetest bliss with cureless pains?
Away, false fear! nor think capricious fate
Would lodge a daemon in a form divine!
Sooner the dove shall seek a tyger mate,
Or the soft snow-drop round the thistle twine;
Yet, yet, I dread to hope, nor dare to hate,
Too proud to sue! too tender to resign!

SONNET XXI.

~~~~~~~~~~~~~~~~

WHY do I live to loath the cheerful day,
To shun the smiles of Fame, and mark the hours
On tardy pinions move, while ceaseless show'rs
Down my wan cheek in lucid currents stray?
My tresses all abound, nor gems display,
Nor scents Arabian! on my path no flow'rs
Imbibe the morn's resuscitating pow'rs,
For one blank sorrow, saddens all my way!
As slow the radiant Sun of reason rose,
Through tears my dying parents saw it shine;
A brother's frailties, swell'd the tide of woes,-
And, keener far, maternal griefs were mine!
Phaon! if soon these weary eyes shall close,
Oh! must that task, that mournful task, be thine?

SONNET XXII.

~~~~~~~~~~~~~~~~

WILD is the foaming Sea! The surges roar!
And nimbly dart the livid lightnings round!
On the rent rock the angry waves rebound;
Ah me! the less'ning bark is seen no more!
Along the margin of the trembling shore,
Loud as the blast my frantic cries shall sound,
My storm-drench'd limbs the flinty fragments wound,
And o'er my bleeding breast the billows pour!
Phaon! return! ye winds, O! waft the strain
To his swift bark; ye barb'rous waves forbear!
Taunt not the anguish of a lover's brain,
Nor feebly emulate the soul's despair!
For howling winds, and foaming seas, in vain
Assail the breast, when passion rages there!

SONNET XXIII

~~~~~~~~~~~~~~~~

TO AEtna's scorching sands my Phaon flies!
False Youth! can other charms attractive prove?
Say, can Sicilian loves thy passions move,
Play round thy heart, and fix thy fickle eyes,
While in despair the Lesbian Sappho dies?
Has Spring for thee a crown of poppies wove,
Or dost thou languish in th' Idalian grove,
Whose altar kindles, fann'd by Lover's sighs?
Ah! think, that while on AEtna's shores you stray,
A fire, more fierce than AEtna's, fills my breast;
Nor deck Sicilian nymphs with garlands gay,
While Sappho's brows with cypress wreaths are drest;
Let one kind word my weary woes repay,
Or, in eternal slumbers bid them rest.

SONNET XXIV

~~~~~~~~~~~~~~~~

O THOU! meek Orb! that stealing o'er the dale
Cheer'st with thy modest beams the noon of night!
On the smooth lake diffusing silv'ry light,
Sublimely still, and beautifully pale!
What can thy cool and placid eye avail,
Where fierce despair absorbs the mental sight,
While inbred glooms the vagrant thoughts invite,
To tempt the gulph where howling fiends assail?
O, Night! all nature owns thy temper'd pow'r;
Thy solemn pause, thy dews, thy pensive beam;
Thy sweet breath whisp'ring in the moonlight bow'r,
While fainting flow'rets kiss the wand'ring stream!
Yet, vain is ev'ry charm! and vain the hour,
That brings to madd'ning love, no soothing dream!

SONNET XXV

~~~~~~~~~~~~~~~~

CAN'ST thou forget, O! Idol of my Soul!
Thy Sappho's voice, her form, her dulcet Lyre!
That melting ev'ry thought to fond desire,
Bade sweet delerium o'er thy senses roll?
Can'st thou, so soon, renounce the blest control
That calm'd with pity's tears love's raging fire,
While Hope, slow breathing on the trembling wire,
In every note with soft persuasion stole?
Oh! Sov'reign of my heart! return! return!
For me no spring appears, no summers bloom,
No Sun-beams glitter, and no altars burn!
The mind's dark winter of eternal gloom,
Shews 'midst the waste a solitary urn,
A blighted laurel, and a mould'ring tomb!

SONNET XXVI

~~~~~~~~~~~~~~~~

WHERE antique woods o'er-hang the mountains's crest,
And mid-day glooms in solemn silence lour;
Philosophy, go seek a lonely bow'r,
And waste life's fervid noon in fancied rest.
Go, where the bird of sorrow weaves her nest,
Cooing, in sadness sweet, through night's dim hour;
Go, cull the dew-drops from each potent flow'r
That med'cines to the cold and reas'ning breast!
Go, where the brook in liquid lapse steals by,
Scarce heard amid'st the mingling echoes round,
What time, the noon fades slowly down the sky,
And slumb'ring zephyrs moan, in caverns bound:
Be these thy pleasures, dull Philosophy!
Nor vaunt the balm, to heal a lover's wound.

SONNET XXVII

~~~~~~~~~~~~~~~~

OH! ye bright Stars! that on the Ebon fields
Of Heav'n's empire, trembling seems to stand;
'Till rosy morn unlocks her portal bland,
Where the proud Sun his fiery banner wields!
To flames, less fierce than mine, your lustre yields,
And pow'rs more strong my countless tears command;
Love strikes the feeling heart with ruthless hand,
And only spares the breast which dullness shields!
Since, then, capricious nature but bestows
The fine affections of the soul, to prove
A keener sense of desolating woes,
Far, far from me the empty boast remove;
If bliss from coldness, pain from passion flows,
Ah! who would wish to feel, or learn to love?

SONNET XXVIII

~~~~~~~~~~~~~~~~

WEAK is the sophistry, and vain the art
That whispers patience to the mind's despair!
That bids reflection bathe the wounds of care,
While Hope, with pleasing phantoms, soothes their smart.
For mem'ry still, reluctant to depart
From the dear spot, once rich in prospects fair,
Bids the fond soul enamour'd there,
And its least charm is grateful to the heart!
He never lov'd, who could not muse and sigh,
Spangling the sacred turf with frequent tears,
Where the small rivulet, that ripples by,
Recalls the scenes of past and happier years,
When, on its banks he watch'd the speaking eye,
And one sweet smile o'erpaid an age of fears!

SONNET XXIX

~~~~~~~~~~~~~~~~

FAREWELL, ye tow'ring Cedars, in whose shade,
Lull'd by the Nightingale, I sunk to rest,
While spicy breezes hover'd o'er my breast
To fan my cheek, in deep'ning tints array'd;
While am'rous insects, humming round me, play'd,
Each flow'r forsook, of prouder sweets in quest;
Of glowing lips, in humid fragrance drest,
That mock'd the Sunny Hybla's vaunted aid!
Farewell, ye limpid rivers! Oh! farewell!
No more shall Sappho to your grots repair;
No more your white waves to her bosom swell,
Or your dank weeds, entwine her floating hair;
As erst, when Venus in her sparry cell
Wept, to behold a brighter goddess there!

SONNET XXX

~~~~~~~~~~~~~~~~

O'ER the tall cliff that bounds the billowy main
Shad'wing the surge that sweeps the lonely strand,
While the thin vapours break along the sand,
Day's harbinger unfolds the liquid plain.
The rude Sea murmurs, mournful as the strain
That love-lorn minstrels strike with trembling hand,
While from their green beds rise the Syren band
With tongues aerial to repeat my pain!
The vessel rocks beside the pebbly shore,
The foamy curls its gaudy trappings lave;
Oh! Bark propitious! bear me gently o'er,
Breathe soft, ye winds; rise slow, O! swelling wave!
Lesbos; these eyes shall meet thy sands no more:
I fly, to seek my Lover, or my Grave!

SONNET XXXI

~~~~~~~~~~~~~~~~

FAR o'er the waves my lofty Bark shall glide,
Love's frequent sighs the flutt'ring sails shall swell,
While to my native home I bid farewell,
Hope's snowy hand the burnis'd helm shall guide!
Triton's shall sport admidst the yielding tide,
Myriads of Cupids round the prow shall dwell,
And Venus, thron'd within her opal shell,
Shall proudly o'er the glitt'ring billows ride!
Young Dolphins, dashing in the golden spray,
Shall with their scaly forms illume the deep
Ting'd with the purple flush of sinking day,
Whose flaming wreath shall crown the distant steep;
While on the breezy deck soft minstrels play,
And songs of love, the lover soothe to sleep!

SONNET XXXII.

~~~~~~~~~~~~~~~~

BLEST as the Gods! Sicilian Maid is he,
The youth whose soul thy yielding graces charm;
Who bound, O! thraldom sweet! by beauty's arm,
In idle dalliance fondly sports with thee!
Blest as the Gods! that iv'ry throne to see,
Throbbing with transports, tender, timid, warm!
While round thy fragrant lips zephyrs swarm!
As op'ning buds attract the wand'ring Bee!
Yet, short is youthful passion's fervid hour;
Soon, shall another clasp the beauteous boy;
Soon, shall a rival prove, in that gay bow'r,
The pleasing torture of excessive joy!
The Bee flies sicken'd from the sweetest flow'r;
The lightning's shaft, but dazzles to destroy!

SONNET XXXIII.

~~~~~~~~~~~~~~~~

I WAKE! delusive phantoms hence, away!
Tempt not the weakness of a lover's breast;
The softest breeze can shake the halcyon's nest,
And lightest clouds o'ercast the dawning ray!
'Twas but a vision! Now, the star of day
Peers, like a gem on Aetna's burning crest!
Wellcome, ye Hills, with golden vintage drest;
Sicilian forests brown, and vallies gay!
A mournful stranger, from the Lesbian Isle,
Not strange, in loftiest eulogy of Song!
She, who could teach the Stoic's cheek to smile,
Thaw the cold heart, and chain the wond'ring throng,
Can find no balm, love's arrows to beguile;
Ah! Sorrows known too soon! and felt too long!

SONNET XXXIV.

~~~~~~~~~~~~~~~~

VENUS! to thee, the Lesbian Muse shall sing,
The song, which Myttellenian youths admir'd,
when Echo, am'rous of the strain inspir'd,
Bade the wild rocks with madd'ning plaudits ring!
Attend my pray'r! O! Queen of rapture! bring
To these fond arms, he, whom my soul has fir'd;
From these fond arms remov'd; yet, still desir'd,
Though love, exulting, spreads his varying wing!
Oh! source of ev'ry joy! of ev'ry care
Blest Venus! Goddess of the zone divine!
To Phaon's bosom, Phaon's victim bear;
So shall her warmest, tend'rest vows be thine!
For Venus, Sappho shall a wreath prepare,
And Love be crown'd, immortal as the Nine!

SONNET XXXV.

~~~~~~~~~~~~~~~~

WHAT means the mist opake that veils these eyes;
Why does yon threat'ning tempest shroud the day?
Why does thy altar, Venus, fade away,
And on my breast the dews of horror rise?
Phaon is false! be dim ye orient Skies;
And let black Erebus succeed your ray;
Let clashing thunders roll, and lightning play;
Phaon is false! and hopeless Sappho dies!
"Farewell! my Lesbian love, you might have said,"
Such sweet remembrance had some pity prov'd,
"Or coldly this, farewell, Oh! Lesbian maid!"
No task severe, for one so fondly lov'd!
The gentle thought had sooth'd my wand'ring shade,
From life's dark valley, and its thorns remov'd!

SONNET XXXVI.

~~~~~~~~~~~~~~~~

LEAD me, Sicilian Maids, to haunted bow'rs,
While yon pale moon displays her faintest beams
O'er blasted woodlands, and enchanted streams,
Whose banks infect the breeze with pois'nous flow'rs.
Ah! lead me, where the barren mountain tow'rs,
Where no sounds echo, but the night-owl's screams,
Where some lone spirit of the desart gleams,
And lurid horrors wing the fateful hours!
Now goaded frenzy grasps my shrinking brain,
Her touch absorbs the crystal fount of woe!
My blood rolls burning through each gasping vein;
Away, lost Lyre! unless thou can'st bestow
A charm, to lull that agonizing pain,
Which those who never lov'd, can never know!

SONNET XXXVII.

~~~~~~~~~~~~~~~~

WHEN, in the gloomy mansion of the dead,
This with'ring heart, this faded form shall sleep;
When these fond eyes, at length shall cease to weep,
And earth's cold lap receive this fev'rish head;
Envy shall turn away, a tear to shed,
And Time's obliterating pinions sweep
The spot, where poets shall their vigils keep,
To mourn and wander near my freezing bed!
Then, my pale ghost, upon th' Elysian shore,
Shall smile, releas'd from ev'ry mortal care;
Whil, doom'd love's victim to repine no more,
My breast shall bathe in endless rapture there!
Ah! no!my restless shade would still deplore,
Nor taste that bliss, which Phaon did not share.

SONNET XXXVIII.

~~~~~~~~~~~~~~~~

OH Sigh! thou steal'st, the herald of the breast,
The lover's fears, the lover's pangs to tell;
Thou bid'st with timid grace the bosom swell,
Cheating the day of joy, the night of rest!
Oh! lucid Tears! with eloquence confest,
Why on my fading cheek unheeded dwell,
Meek, as the dew-drops on the flowret's bell
By ruthless tempests to the green-sod prest.
Fond sigh be hush'd! congeal, O! slighted tear!
Thy feeble pow'rs the busy Fates control!
Or if thy crystal streams again appear,
Let them, like Lethe's, oblivion roll:
For Love the tyrant plays, when hope is near,
And she who flies the lover, chains the soul!

SONNET XXXIX.

~~~~~~~~~~~~~~~~

PREPARE your wreaths, Aonian maids divine,
To strew the tranquil bed where I shall sleep;
In tears, the myrtle and the laurel steep,
And let Erato's hand the trophies twine.
No parian marble, there, with labour'd line,
Shall bid the wand'ring lover stay to weep;
There holy silence shall her vigils keep.
Save, when the nightingale such woes as mine
Shall sadly sing; as twilight's curtains spread,
There shall the branching lotos widely wave,
Sprinkling soft show'rs upon the lily's head,
Sweet drooping emblem for a lover's grave!
And there shall Phaon pearls of pity shed,
To gem the vanquish'd heart he scorn'd to save!

SONNET XL.

~~~~~~~~~~~~~~~~

ON the low margin of a murm'ring stream,
As rapt in meditation's arms I lay;
Each aching sense in slumbers stole away,
While potent fancy form'd a soothing dream;
O'er the Leucadian deep, a dazzling beam
Shed the bland light of empyrean day!
But soon transparent shadows veil'd each ray,
While mystic visions sprang athwart the gleam!
Now to the heaving gulf they seem'd to bend,
And now across the sphery regions glide;
Now in mid-air, their dulcet voices blend,
"Awake! awake!" the restless phalanx cried,
"See ocean yawns the lover's woes to end,
"Plunge the green wave, and bid thy griefs subside."

SONNET XLI.

~~~~~~~~~~~~~~~~

YES, I will go, where circling whirlwinds rise,
Where threat'ning clouds in sable grandeur lour;
Where the blast yells, the liquid columns pour,
And madd'ning billows combat with the skies!
There, while the Daemon of the tempest flies
On growing pinions through the troublous hour,
The wild waves gasp impatient to devour,
And on the rock the waken'd Vulture cries!
Oh! dreadful solace to the stormy mind!
To me, more pleasing than the valley's rest,
The woodland songsters, or the sportive kind,
That nip the turf, or prune the painted crest;
For in despair alone, the wretched find
That unction sweet, which lulls the bleeding breast!

SONNET XLII.

~~~~~~~~~~~~~~~~

OH! can'st thou bear to see this faded frame,
Deform'd and mangled by the rocky deep?
Wilt thou remember, and forbear to weep,
My fatal fondness, and my peerless fame?
Soon o'er this heart, now warm with passion's flame,
The howling winds and foamy waves shall sweep;
Those eyes be ever clos'd in death's cold sleep,
And all of Sappho perish, but her name!
Yet, if the Fates suspend their barb'rous ire,
If days less mournful, Heav'n designs for me!
If rocks grow kind, and winds and waves conspire,
To bear me softly on the swelling sea;
To Phoebus only will I tune my Lyre,
"What suits with Sappho, Phoebus suits with thee!"

SONNET XLIII.

~~~~~~~~~~~~~~~~

WHILE from the dizzy precipice I gaze,
The world receding from my pensive eyes,
High o'er my head the tyrant eagle flies,
Cloth'd in the sinking sun's transcendent blaze!
The meek-ey'd moon, 'midst clouds of amber plays
As o'er the purpling plains of light she hies,
Till the last stream of living lustre dies,
And the cool concave owns her temper'd rays!
So shall this glowing, palpitating soul,
Welcome returning Reason's placid beam,
While o'er my breast the waves Lethean roll,
To calm rebellious Fancy's fev'rish dream;
Then shall my Lyre disdain love's dread control,
And loftier passions, prompt the loftier theme!

SONNET XLIV. CONCLUSIVE.

~~~~~~~~~~~~~~~~

HERE droops the muse! while from her glowing mind,
Celestial Sympathy, with humid eye,
Bids the light Sylph capricious Fancy fly,
Time's restless wings with transient flowr's to bind!
For now, with folded arms and head inclin'd,
Reflection pours the deep and frequent sigh,
O'er the dark scroll of human destiny,
Where gaudy buds and wounding thorns are twin'd.
O! Sky-born VIRTUE! sacred is thy name!
And though mysterious Fate, with frown severe,
Oft decorates thy brows with wreaths of Fame,
Bespangled o'er with sorrow's chilling tear!
Yet shalt thou more than mortal raptures claim,
The brightest planet of th' ETERNAL SPHERE!

FINIS.

Lightning Source UK Ltd.
Milton Keynes UK
UKOW04f0514110915

258411UK00003B/322/P